Quick Start Guides

The Essential
SUGAR FREE
DESSERTS
RECIPE BOOK

A Quick Start Guide To Cooking Sugar-Free Cakes, Desserts and Sweet Treats

Over 80 Sweet And Delicious Sugar-Free Recipes To Make Quitting Sugar Easy

First published in 2016 by Erin Rose Publishing

Text and illustration copyright © 2016 Erin Rose Publishing

Design: Julie Anson

ISBN: 978-1-911492-02-3

A CIP record for this book is available from the British Library.

DISCLAIMER: This book is for informational purposes only and not intended as a substitute for the medical advice, diagnosis or treatment of a physician or qualified healthcare provider. The reader should consult a physician before undertaking a new health care regime and in all matters relating to his/her health, and particularly with respect to any symptoms that may require diagnosis or medical attention.

While every care has been taken in compiling the recipes for this book we cannot accept responsibility for any problems which arise as a result of preparing one of the recipes. The author and publisher disclaim responsibility for any adverse effects that may arise from the use or application of the recipes in this book. Some of the recipes in this book include nuts and eggs. If you have an egg or nut allergy it's important to avoid these.

CONTENTS

INTRODUCTION

Anyone starting a sugar-free diet, even reformed sugaraholics, will know those sneaky cravings for something sweet can be a diet-breaker if you give in to the temptation of a chocolate dessert. The number one reason we break our healthy sugar-free diet is because we are too tempted by sweets, desserts and cakes which are loaded with refined sugar. So, if your greatest challenge to your healthy diet is how to avoid the lure of the white stuff and you want to satisfy sugar-cravings with a healthy sweet tasting dessert or snack, then this is the book for you!

The benefits of cutting out sugar from your diet are well known. Thankfully, we have taken a big step towards better health, and that millions of people worldwide are now avoiding the sugar, revolutionising the way we eat – not just cutting out the obvious sugars but the hidden sugars in everyday foods too!

In this book we bring you plenty of simple and delicious sugar-free recipes for sweet tasting snacks and desserts, satisfying your taste buds with something tasty from the wide selection of cookies, cakes, pudding and chocolatey delights and making healthy eating easier. There is something for everyone, from traditional family favourites to innovative energy balls, desserts and brownies, using natural sweetness and low carb ingredients.

Whether you are avoiding refined sugar, honey and syrups, steering clear of too much fructose or even starting a low-carb diet, you'll find something to suit you from over 80 simply mouth-watering recipes. Healthy eating is now easier and delicious!

Cakes

Chocolate Cheesecake

Ingredients

FOR THE BASE:

125g (4oz) butter

75g (3oz) ground almonds (almond meal/almond flour)

50g (2oz) pecan nuts

4 tablespoons 100% cocoa powder

3 teaspoons stevia powder (or to taste)

2 tablespoons coconut oil

2 large eggs

1 teaspoon vanilla extract

FOR THE FILLING:

450g (1lb) ricotta cheese

4 teaspoons stevia sweetener

2 large eggs

1 teaspoon vanilla extract

60mls (2oz) double cream (heavy cream)

SERVES 8-10

Method

Grease and line a spring form baking tin. Place the butter, coconut oil and cocoa powder into a saucepan and stir until the butter has melted. Remove it from the heat. In a bowl, combine the eggs, stevia and vanilla and mix well. Stir in the chocolate mixture, nuts and ground almonds (almond flour/almond meal) and combine the ingredients. Spoon the mixture into the baking tin and press it into the edges. Transfer it to the oven and bake at 170C/325F for 15 minutes. Remove it and allow it to cool. In a bowl combine the ingredients for the filling and beat until smooth and creamy. Spread the filling over the top of the base. Transfer it to the oven and bake at 150C/300F for 40 minutes or until the cheesecake has completely set. Remove it from the oven and allow it to cool. Chill before serving.

Pineapple Cream Cake

Ingredients

FOR THE BASE:
225g (8oz) ground almonds (almond flour/almond meal)
3 tablespoons coconut oil or vegetable oil
2 tablespoons water
Pinch of salt

FOR THE FILLING:
450g (1lb) tinned crushed pineapple, in own juice (unsweetened)
Pinch of salt
1 teaspoon stevia sweetener (optional)
400mls (14fl oz) full-fat coconut milk

SERVES 8

Method

Place the almonds, oil, water and salt into a bowl and combine them. Press the mixture into a spring form baking tin. Transfer it to the oven and bake at 170C/350F for 15 minutes. Allow it to cool. Pour the coconut milk into a food processor, add the pineapple and stevia and blend the ingredients together. Scoop the pineapple mixture on top of the base. Place it in the freezer until frozen. Defrost it before serving chilled.

Cinnamon & Walnut Mug Cake

Ingredients

- 2 teaspoons ground flaxseeds (linseeds)
- 2 tablespoons ground almonds (almond meal/almond flour)
- 1 tablespoon chopped walnuts
- 1 egg
- 1/2 teaspoon vanilla extract
- 1/2 teaspoon baking powder
- 1/2 teaspoon cinnamon
- 1/4 teaspoon stevia (or to taste)
- 1 teaspoon coconut oil
- Pinch of salt

SERVES
1

Method

Place all the ingredients, except the walnuts, into a large mug or a microwaveable bowl and mix well. Cook in the microwave for 30 seconds, remove and stir then return it to the microwave for another 30 seconds, remove and stir in the walnuts. Return it to the microwave for another 30 seconds. Chill in the fridge before serving. Serve and enjoy.

Strawberry & Lime Mug Cheesecake

SERVES 1

Ingredients

50g (2oz) cream cheese
25g (1oz) strawberries
2 tablespoons crème fraîche

1 egg
1 teaspoon lemon juice
1/2 teaspoon vanilla extract
1/2 teaspoon stevia extract (or to taste)

Method

Place all the ingredients, except the strawberries, into a large mug or a microwaveable bowl and mix well. Cook in the microwave for 30 seconds, remove and stir then return it to the microwave for another 30 seconds, remove and stir. Return it to the microwave for another 30 seconds. Chill in the fridge before serving. Serve with a scattering of blueberries.

Vanilla Cupcakes

Ingredients

200g (7oz) butter
125g (4oz) self-raising flour
3 teaspoons stevia sweetener
2 large eggs
1 teaspoon vanilla extract

MAKES
12

Method

Place the butter and stevia into a bowl and beat until smooth and creamy. Add the eggs and vanilla extract to the mixture and mix well. Sieve the flour into the wet mixture and combine. Place paper cases into a muffin tin and spoon some of the mixture into each one. Transfer to the oven, preheated to 180C/360F and bake for 10 minutes until slightly golden. Remove them and allow them to cool. This recipe for basic cupcake mixture can be livened up by adding unsweetened chocolate chips or topping them off with a swirl of cream cheese and a strawberry. Experiment and find your favourite.

Chocolate Cupcakes

Ingredients

- 125g (4oz) ground almonds (almond meal/almond flour)
- 2 eggs
- 2 tablespoons ground linseeds (flaxseeds)
- 1 tablespoon peanut butter or almond butter
- 1 tablespoon 100% cocoa powder
- ½ butternut squash, cooked and mashed
- ½ teaspoon bicarbonate of soda/baking soda
- 60mls (2fl oz) coconut oil (melted)

MAKES 6

Method

In a bowl, stir together the ground almonds (almond meal/almond flour), flaxseeds (linseeds) bicarbonate of soda (baking soda) and cocoa powder. Add the eggs to the mixture and combine. In a separate bowl, mix the squash, coconut oil and nut butter. Stir the squash mixture into the dry ingredients and mix well. Spoon the mixture into a 6 hole muffin tin and transfer to the oven. Bake at 180C/350F for 30 minutes. Test with a skewer which will come out clean when they're cooked.

Orange Cream Cupcakes

Ingredients

FOR THE CUPCAKES:

175g (6oz) ground almonds (almond meal/almond flour)

75g (3oz) butter, softened

5 eggs, separated

4-5 teaspoons stevia sweetener (or to taste)

2 teaspoons baking powder

1/4 teaspoon of cream of tartar

3 tablespoons orange juice

FOR THE TOPPING:

175g (6oz) cream cheese

Zest of 1 orange

4 teaspoons stevia sweetener

**MAKES
10 approx**

Method

Place the ground almonds (almond flour/almond meal) and baking powder in a bowl and mix well. In a separate bowl combine the egg yolks, butter, orange juice and stevia and mix well. In a separate bowl whisk the egg whites together with the cream of tartar until if forms stiff peaks. Slowly fold the egg whites into the egg yolk mixture until gently combined. Fold in the almond mixture until well combined. Spoon the mixture into cupcake papers. Transfer to the oven and bake at 180C/360F and cook for around 25 minutes. Test the cupcakes with a skewer which should come out clean. Allow them to cool. In a bowl, beat the cream cheese together with the stevia and orange zest and mix thoroughly. Spread some topping onto each of the cooled cupcakes.

Banana Bread

Ingredients

250g (9 oz) plain flour (all-purpose flour)
125g (4oz) butter, softened
50g (2oz) walnuts, chopped (optional)
3 medium eggs
2 ripe bananas, mashed
2 teaspoons bicarbonate of soda
175mls (6fl oz) water

SERVES 6

Method

Place the bananas and butter into a large bowl and combine them until the mixture is creamy. Add in the eggs and mix well. Add in the flour, bicarbonate of soda (baking soda), baking powder to the banana mixture. Slowly add in the water and beat the mixture well then stir in the walnuts (if using). Transfer the mixture into a greased baking tin. Transfer it to the oven, preheated to 180C/360F and cook for 35 minutes. Allow it to cool before cutting it into slices.

Black Forest Berry Cake

Ingredients

375g (13oz) plain flour (all-purpose flour)

250g (9oz) fresh mixed fruit (cherries, strawberries, blackberries, raspberries or blueberries)

175g (6oz) butter, softened

4-5 teaspoons stevia sweetener (or to taste)

2 teaspoons baking powder

250mls (8fl oz) freshly whipped cream

250mls (8fl oz) milk

3 eggs

1 teaspoon vanilla extract

SERVES 12

Method

Place the flour, baking powder and stevia into a bowl and mix well. In a separate bowl combine the butter, eggs, milk and vanilla and beat until smooth and creamy. Fold the dry ingredients into the bowl of wet ingredients and combine them. Add in the fruit and mix well. Spoon the mixture equally into two baking tins. Transfer them to the oven and bake at 180C/360F and cook for around 25 minutes or until cooked through. Test the mixture using a skewer which should come out clean when it's done. Allow them to cool on a wire rack. Once completely cool, turn one cake upside down on a serving plate and cover it in whipped cream. Place the other cake on top. Garnish with a swirl of cream and extra berries, if you wish.

Fresh Apricot Muffins

Ingredients

125g (4oz) coconut flour
100g (3½oz) apricots, stone removed
and chopped
3 eggs, whisked
2 ripe bananas, mashed
4 tablespoons coconut oil
1 teaspoon vanilla extract
½ teaspoon baking powder
Pinch of salt

**MAKES
12**

Method

Place the eggs and bananas into a bowl and beat them until creamy. Place the coconut flour in a separate bowl and add in the baking powder, coconut oil, vanilla extract and a pinch of salt and mix well. Add in the egg mixture and combine until smooth. Add in the chopped apricots and mix well. Line a 12 muffin tin with paper cases and scoop some mixture into each one. Transfer them to the oven and bake at 200C/400F for 20 minutes or until cooked through and slightly golden.

Blueberry Breakfast Muffins

Ingredients

200g (7oz) wholemeal self-raising flour
175g (6oz) blueberries
50g (2oz) porridge oats
1½ teaspoons bicarbonate of soda (baking soda)
2-3 teaspoons stevia sweetener (or to taste)
2 ripe bananas, mashed
1 egg
100mls (3½fl oz) milk or almond milk

MAKES 12

Method

Place the flour, oats, stevia and bicarbonate of soda (baking soda) into a bowl. In a separate bowl, mix together the mashed banana and egg. Add in the milk and mix well. Add the flour mixture into the wet mixture and mix well until there are no bits of flour or oats uncoated. Stir in the blueberries. Spoon the mixture into a 12-hole muffin tin. Transfer them to the oven and bake at 180C/360F for 20 minutes until slightly golden. Test the muffins with a skewer which should come out clean when they are cooked. Set them on a wire rack to cool.

Baked Chocolate Orange Cheesecake

Ingredients

800g (1¾ lb) cream cheese, such as mascarpone

4 eggs

4 tablespoons orange juice

3 tablespoons 100% cocoa powder

2 teaspoons stevia (or to taste)

SERVES
8 approx

Method

Place all of the ingredients into a bowl and mix thoroughly. Transfer the mixture to a pie dish and bake at 170C/325F for one hour. Remove the cheesecake and allow it to cool. Chill before serving.

Low Carb Blueberry & Almond Cake

Ingredients

125g (4oz) ground almonds (almond meal/ almond flour)

125g (4oz) blueberries (raspberries also work well)

4 medium eggs

2 teaspoons baking powder

2 teaspoons stevia powder (or to taste)

3 tablespoons olive oil

2 teaspoons vanilla extract

SERVES 8

Method

Place the almonds, eggs, baking powder, stevia, oil and vanilla extract into a bowl and mix really well. Stir in the blueberries. Grease and line a small loaf tin with greaseproof paper. Transfer it to the oven and bake at 200C/400F for 20 minutes. This cake won't rise very much. Test it with a skewer which should come out clean. Allow to cool. Store in an airtight container.

Carrot Cake & Orange Icing

Ingredients

- 300g (11oz) carrots, grated (shredded)
- 150g (5oz) self-raising flour
- 100g (3½ oz) ground almonds (almond meal/almond flour)
- 50g (2oz) walnuts, chopped
- 2 teaspoons ground mixed spice
- 3 eggs
- 3 teaspoons stevia powder
- 1 teaspoon bicarbonate of soda (baking soda)
- 100ml (3½ oz) sunflower oil
- 3 tablespoons milk

FOR THE ICING:
- 150g (5oz) soft cheese
- Grated zest of 1 orange

SERVES 12

Method

Place the flour, walnuts, spice, bicarbonate of soda (baking soda) and stevia into a bowl and mix well. In a separate bowl, mix together the carrots, milk, eggs and oil. Pour the milk mixture into the flour mixture and combine well until thick and creamy. Grease and line a baking tin with greaseproof paper. Pour the mixture into the baking tin and cook in the oven preheated to 180C/360F and cook for around 55 minutes. Test if it's cooked by using a skewer which should come out clean. Allow the cake to cool. Place it on a serving plate. In a bowl, mix together the orange zest and cream cheese. Spread the mixture onto the carrot cake. Slice, serve and enjoy.

Apple & Cinnamon Muffins

Ingredients

- 225g (8oz) apple, peeled and finely chopped
- 175g (6oz) plain flour (all-purpose flour)
- 100g (3½ oz) butter, softened
- 50g (2oz) ground almonds (almond meal/almond flour)
- 1 teaspoon bicarbonate of soda (baking soda)
- 2 teaspoons cream of tartar
- 1 teaspoon stevia sweetener (or to taste)
- 1 teaspoon ground cinnamon
- 2 eggs

MAKES 12

Method

Place the butter and stevia sweetener into a food processor and blitz until smooth.
Add in the ground almonds (almond meal/almond flour), flour, bicarbonate of soda
(baking soda), cream of tartar, eggs and cinnamon and blitz until smooth. Add around
¾ of the apple and process. Stir in the remaining chopped apple. Transfer the mixture to
a 12 hole muffin tin. Bake in the oven preheated to 180C/360F for 20 minutes. Test the
muffins with a skewer which should come out clean. Allow them to cool. Store in
an airtight container.

Strawberry & Cream Scones

Ingredients

250 (9 oz) self raising flour
2 teaspoons stevia sweetener
50g (2oz) butter
200mls (7fl oz) milk

FOR THE TOPPING:
150g (5oz) fresh ripe strawberries, chopped
250mls (8fl oz) double cream (heavy cream)

MAKES 12

Method

Place the flour and stevia in a bowl and stir. Cut flakes of butter into the flour and using clean hands, rub it into the flour. Pour in the milk and mix to a dough. Grease and line a baking sheet. Scatter some flour onto a work surface and roll out the scone mixture to 2cm (1 inch) thick. Use a cookie cutter and cut into rounds. Place them onto the baking sheet and coat them with some extra milk. Transfer them to the oven, preheated to 180C/360F for around 20 minutes or until golden. Allow them to cool. Whisk the double cream until thick. When ready to serve, cut the scones in half, dollop some cream on top and scatter chopped strawberries onto the cream. Enjoy!

Fruit Cake

Ingredients

250g (9 oz) self-raising flour
200g (7oz) sultanas
75g (3oz) carrots, grated (shredded)
50g (2oz) dates, chopped
2 eggs
1 large apple, peeled, cored and chopped
1 teaspoon baking powder
1/2 teaspoon ground cinnamon
1/2 teaspoon ground nutmeg
250mls (8fl oz) hot water (for soaking)
100mls (3 1/2fl oz) vegetable oil

SERVES 8

Method

Soak the sultanas and dates in a bowl of hot water for around 10 minutes. Drain off all the water. Grease and line a cake tin, around 18cm (7 inches) with greaseproof paper. Place the flour, baking powder, cinnamon, and nutmeg into a bowl and stir. Add in the eggs and oil and mix well. Stir in the apple, carrots, dates and sultanas. Pour the mixture into the prepared baking tin. Transfer it to the oven and bake at 180C/360F and cook for 45 minutes. Test the cake with a skewer which should come out clean when it is completely cooked.

Quick Low-Carb Raspberry Cheesecake

SERVES 2

Ingredients

200g (8oz) raspberries
200g (8oz) mascarpone cheese
75g (3oz) ground almonds (almond flour/almond meal)
1 tablespoon 100% cocoa powder

Method

Heat the raspberries in a saucepan until warmed through then set aside to cool. Sprinkle the ground almonds (almond flour/almond meal) onto the bottom of two serving bowls. Place the mascarpone cheese in a bowl, add in the cocoa powder and mix until smooth and well combined. Spoon the mixture on top of the almond base. Once the raspberries are cool, serve them on top. Enjoy.

Brownies and Biscuits

Raspberry & Chocolate Brownies

Ingredients

200g (7oz) self-raising flour (all-purpose flour)
100g (3½oz) butter
100g (3½oz) raspberries
50g (2oz) 100% cocoa powder
25g (1oz) cacao nibs or unsweetened chocolate chips
3 large free-range eggs, beaten
2 ripe bananas, mashed
1 teaspoon bicarbonate of soda
100mls (3½ fl oz) milk

MAKES 16 approx.

Method

In a bowl, mix together the flour, cocoa powder and bicarbonate of soda. Gently melt the butter in a saucepan, remove it from the heat and add in the bananas, milk and eggs and mix quickly. Pour the egg mixture into the flour mixture and mix thoroughly. Stir in the raspberries. Grease and line a baking tin with greaseproof paper. Scoop the brownie mixture into the baking tin. Scatter the cacao nibs/ chocolate chips over the mixture. Transfer it to the oven, preheated to 180C/360F and bake for around 30 minutes. Allow it to cool before cutting into squares.

Banana & Walnut Brownies

Ingredients

- 200g (7oz) self-raising flour
- 100g (3½oz) butter
- 50g (2oz) 100% cocoa powder
- 25g (1oz) walnuts, chopped
- 3 large eggs, beaten
- 3 ripe bananas, mashed
- 1 teaspoon bicarbonate of soda (baking soda)
- 100mls (3½fl oz) milk

MAKES
16 approx.

Method

In a bowl, mix the flour, cocoa powder and bicarbonate of soda (baking soda). Gently melt the butter in a saucepan, remove it from the heat and add in the bananas, milk and eggs and mix quickly. Pour the egg mixture into the dry ingredients and combine them thoroughly. Stir in the walnuts. Grease and line a baking tin with greaseproof paper. Spoon the mixture into the tin. Transfer it to the oven, preheated to 180C/360F and bake for around 30 minutes. Test it with a skewer which should come out clean when it's completely cooked. Allow it to cool before cutting into squares. These are delicious served warm with a dollop of cream.

Lemon Cheese Biscuits

MAKES 12

Ingredients

75g (3oz) finely ground oats

50g (2oz) mascarpone cheese

3 teaspoons stevia powder (or to taste)

Zest and juice of ½ lemon

2 teaspoons vegetable oil

1 teaspoon vanilla extract

Method

Place the mascarpone in a bowl with the stevia, lemon zest, lemon juice, vanilla and vegetable oil. Stir in the oats and combine all of the ingredients until it becomes doughy. Scoop out spoonfuls of the mixture, shape them into balls and flatten them on a baking tray. Transfer them to the oven and bake at 170C/325F for 10 minutes. Allow to cool. Serve and enjoy.

Banana Biscuits

MAKES 20

Ingredients

50g (2oz) butter, melted
50g (2oz) oats
50g (2oz) ground almonds (almond flour/almond meal)
25g (1oz) ground linseeds (flaxseeds)
2 ripe bananas
1 teaspoon vanilla extract

Method

Mash up the bananas in a large bowl and mix with the melted butter and vanilla. Add all of the remaining ingredients and combine. Leave to stand for 10 minutes and the mixture will firm up. Use a teaspoon to scoop out the dough. Roll it into balls and then pat down on a lined baking tray. Bake at 180C/360F for 15-20 minutes or until golden brown.

Peanut Butter Brownies

Ingredients

- 150g (5oz) ground almonds (almond meal/almond flour)
- 125g (4oz) butter
- 75g (3oz) smooth peanut butter
- 50g (2oz) 100% cocoa powder
- 50g (2oz) coconut flour
- 50g (2oz) cacao nibs or unsweetened chocolate chips
- 2 large eggs
- 2 large egg yolks
- 2 teaspoons vanilla extract
- 3-4 teaspoons stevia sweetener (or to taste)
- 150mls (5fl oz) hot water
- 60mls (2fl oz) melted coconut oil

MAKES 16

Method

In a bowl, whisk the hot water, cacao nibs and cocoa powder until the chocolate has melted. Stir in the butter and coconut oil, eggs and yolks, stevia and vanilla and whisk it well. Stir in the ground almonds (almond meal/almond flour) and coconut flour. Spoon the mixture into a square, greased and lined baking tin. Using the tip of a teaspoon, drop little blobs of peanut butter over the top of the mixture then using the tip of a skewer or knife make a swirly pattern with the peanut butter. Transfer it to the oven and bake at 180C/360F and cook for 20 minutes. Allow to cool before cutting into squares. Store in an airtight container.

Low Carb Chocolate Biscuits

MAKES
16 approx.

Ingredients

225g (8oz) tinned chickpeas (garbanzo beans)

125g (4oz) smooth peanut butter

3 tablespoons 100% cocoa powder

1 teaspoon vanilla extract

1 teaspoon stevia sweetener

1 teaspoon baking powder

200mls (7fl oz) soya milk or almond milk

Method

Place all of the ingredients into a blender and process until smooth and creamy. If the mixture seems too thick try adding a little extra milk. Scoop out a spoonful of the mixture and place it on a greased baking tray. Repeat for the remaining mixture. Place it in the oven, preheated to 200C/400F and cook for 15 minutes.

Double Choc Chip Cookies

Ingredients

350g (12oz) plain flour (all-purpose flour)
250g (9oz) butter
100g (3½oz) 100% cocoa powder
25g (1oz) cacao nibs or sugar-free chocolate chips
4 teaspoons stevia sweetener
2 eggs
1 teaspoon bicarbonate of soda

MAKES
20 approx.

Method

Place the butter and stevia powder in a bowl and mix until light and creamy. Add in the eggs and mix well. Sieve in the flour, cocoa powder and bicarbonate of soda (baking soda) and mix the ingredients for form a dough. Stir in the cacao nibs/chocolate chips. Dust a flat surface with flour and roll out the dough. Use a cooker cutter to cut it into the shapes. Grease a baking sheet and lay the biscuits onto it. Transfer to the oven and bake at 180C/360F for around 15 minutes or until golden. Allow to cool. Store in an airtight container.

Pecan Nut & Cinnamon Biscuits

Ingredients

- 125g (4½oz) plain (all-purpose flour)
- 125g (4½oz) butter
- 50g (2oz) pecan nuts
- 2 teaspoons stevia sweetener
- 1 teaspoon vanilla extract
- 1 egg, beaten
- ½ teaspoon bicarbonate of soda (baking powder)
- ½ teaspoon cinnamon

MAKES
16 approx.

146
calories
per serving

Method

Place the flour, stevia, cinnamon and bicarbonate of soda (baking powder) into a bowl. Beat in the butter, vanilla extract and egg and mix until creamy. Stir in the pecan nuts. Line a baking sheet with greaseproof paper. Take out a spoonful of the mixture and using clean hands, roll it into balls. Place the balls on the baking sheet and press them down using the back of a spoon. Transfer them to the oven and bake at 180C/360F and cook for 10 minutes. Allow them to cool before serving.

Spiced Oat Biscuits

Ingredients

150g (5oz) butter
100g (3½oz) rolled oats
4 teaspoons stevia sweetener
1 teaspoon ground allspice
Pinch of salt

MAKES 10

Method

Place the butter and stevia into a saucepan a stir until melted. Place the oats, allspice and salt into a bowl and pour in the butter. Using clean hands, shape the mixture into balls. Grease a baking sheet and flatten the balls onto the baking sheet. Transfer to the oven and bake at 180C/360F for around 15 minutes or until the biscuits are golden. Remove them from the oven and allow them to cool. Store in an airtight container.

Fudgey Blackbean Brownies

Ingredients

- 400g (14oz) tin of black beans, rinsed and drained
- 75g (3oz) cocoa powder
- 50g (2oz) cacao nibs or dark chocolate chips
- 2 egg whites
- 1 large egg
- 1 ripe avocado
- 2-3 teaspoons stevia sweetener
- 1/2 teaspoon cinnamon
- 1/2 teaspoon bicarbonate of soda (baking powder)
- 1/2 teaspoon salt
- 2 teaspoons pure vanilla extract
- 2 teaspoons olive oil

MAKES 12

Method

Place all of the ingredients, except the cacao nibs/chocolate chips, into a blender and process until soft and smooth. If the mixture seems too thick, just add a teaspoon or two or water. Stir in the cacao nibs/ dark chocolate chips. Grease and line a baking tin and pour in the mixture. Transfer it to an oven preheated to 180C/360F for around 25 minutes. Allow it to cool before cutting into bars.

Strawberry & Banana Cookie Bars

MAKES 12

Ingredients

3 medium-sized ripe bananas

150g (5oz) fresh strawberries, stalk removed and chopped

150g (5oz) plain flour (all-purpose flour)

100g (3½oz) butter

3 ripe bananas

1 egg

1 teaspoon baking powder

1 teaspoon vanilla extract

Method

In a bowl, mash the bananas and then whisk in the egg. Melt the butter until it becomes liquid and add it to the banana mixture together with the vanilla extract. Stir in the strawberries. Sieve in the baking powder and flour and mix to a smooth dough. Transfer the mixture to a rectangular baking tin. Transfer to the oven, preheated to 180C/360F and cook for around 10 minutes or until golden. Allow it to cool. Cut into bars and store in an airtight container.

Ginger Biscuits

Ingredients

250g (9oz) plain flour (all-purpose flour)
150g (5oz) butter
2 teaspoons bicarbonate of soda (baking powder)
1 tablespoon ground ginger
1 teaspoon ground cinnamon
1 egg
Pinch of salt

MAKES 12

Method

Place the flour, bicarbonate of soda, ginger, cinnamon and salt into a bowl and mix well. Heat the butter in a saucepan and allow to cool before beating the egg in with the butter. Slowly add the liquid to the dry ingredients. Grease a baking sheet and using clean hands, shape the mixture into balls. Flatten the balls into biscuit shapes on the baking sheet. Alternatively, roll out the mixture and using a cookie cutter, cut the dough into the required size. Transfer to the oven and bake at 180C/360F for around 10 minutes until golden. Allow them to cool. Remove and store in an airtight container.

Vanilla Shortbread

Ingredients

200g (7oz) plain flour (all-purpose flour)
150g (5oz) butter, softened
4 teaspoons stevia powder
2 teaspoons vanilla extract

MAKES
8-10

Method

Place the butter, vanilla extract and stevia into a bowl and beat until light and creamy. Stir in the flour and mix to a dough. Dust a flat surface with a little flour and roll out the shortbread mixture to around 2cm (approx. 1 inch) thick. Use a cookie cutter to cut it into rounds. Grease a baking sheet and place the shortbread on the sheet. Transfer to the oven, preheated to 180C/360F and cook for around 20 minutes or until golden. Allow to cool before serving. You can even try adding chopped nuts or cacao nibs or cocoa powder to this recipe.

Energy Balls & Healthy Snack Bars

Chocolate Red Velvet Bars

Ingredients

250g (9 oz) beetroot, peeled, boiled & cooled
50g (2oz) coconut flour
50g (2oz) buckwheat flour
50g (2oz) cacao nibs/unsweetened chocolate chips
3 eggs
2 large ripe bananas, mashed
2 tablespoons 100% cocoa powder
1 teaspoon ground cinnamon
1 teaspoon bicarbonate of soda (baking powder)
2 tablespoons coconut oil, melted
2 teaspoons vanilla extract
Pinch of salt
FOR THE TOPPING:
50g (2oz) cacao nibs or unsweetened chocolate chips
1 teaspoon stevia sweetener

MAKES 14

Method

Grease and line a baking tin then set it aside. Place the cooked beetroot into a food processor and blend to until smooth. Add in the eggs, banana, coconut oil and vanilla extract and combine them. Place the coconut flour, buckwheat flour, cinnamon, bicarbonate of soda (baking powder) cocoa powder and cacao nibs/chocolate chips and a pinch of salt into a bowl and mix well. Stir in the beetroot and wet ingredients. Transfer the mixture to a baking tin and place it in the oven at 170C/325F for 30 minutes. Allow it to cool before cutting it into bars. Melt the cacao nibs/chocolate chips for the coating into a bowl over gently simmering water. Stir in the stevia sweetener and mix until completely melted. Drizzle the chocolate over the bars and allow them to cool. Store in an airtight container.

Chocolate Cashew Bars

Ingredients

125g (4oz) medjool dates
150g (5oz) unsalted cashews
50g (2oz) 100% cocoa powder
1/2 teaspoon peppermint extract
2 tablespoons almond milk
Pinch of salt

MAKES 12

Method

Place all of the ingredients into a food processor and process until everything is well combined and a soft smooth texture. Spoon the mixture into a rectangular baking tin. Cover the mixture and chill it in the fridge for around 1 hours before cutting it into bars. Serve and eat straight away or stored them in an airtight container. If you wish to add extra protein to this recipe you can add a scoopful of your favourite protein powder to the ingredients.

Pumpkin Seed Bars

Ingredients

125g (4oz) almonds, roughly chopped
100g (3½oz) peanut butter
75g (3oz) pumpkin seeds, raw and unsalted
75g (3oz) sunflower seeds
50g (2oz) oats
50g (2oz) brazil nuts, roughly chopped
1 banana, mashed
1 teaspoon ground cinnamon
3 tablespoons raw honey
Pinch of sea salt

MAKES 16

Method

Place the honey and peanut butter into a saucepan and gently warm it until it melts then remove it from the heat. Place the oats, almonds, brazil nuts, pumpkin seeds, sunflower seeds, cinnamon and salt into a bowl and mix well. Add the peanut butter mixture and banana into the dry ingredients and mix well. Grease and line a square baking tin with parchment paper. Spoon the mixture into the tin, pressing it into the edges. Transfer it to the oven and bake at 180C/360F for 15-20 minutes. Allow them to cool before cutting into bars. Enjoy.

Coconut Protein Bars

Ingredients

200g (8oz) desiccated coconut (shredded)

1 teaspoon vanilla extract

2-3 teaspoons stevia powder

4 tablespoons coconut oil

Pinch of salt

MAKES 12

Method

Place all of the ingredients into a food processor and blitz until smooth. Line a square baking tin with parchment paper. Scoop the mixture into the tin and smooth it out to the corners. Transfer it to the fridge and chill for 1-2 hours. Cut it into 12 slices. Keep them in an airtight container in the fridge until ready to serve. As an alternative you can top the coconut bars with melted dark chocolate before they are ready to be chilled, making your very own bounty bars.

Chocolate Dipped Quinoa Bars

MAKES
20 approx.

Ingredients

150g (5½oz) quinoa, uncooked

150g (5½oz) oats

125g (4oz) peanut butter

100g (3½oz) dark chocolate min 75% cacao

3 teaspoons stevia sweetener

Method

Scatter the oats and quinoa onto a baking sheet. Place it in the oven at 180C/360F for 7 minutes, stirring halfway through. Place the stevia and peanut butter into a bowl and microwave it until melted (or alternatively heat it in a saucepan). Place the oats and quinoa into a bowl and mix it well. Pour the peanut butter mixture into the dry ingredients and combine them. Grease and line a baking tin. Scoop the mixture into the baking tin, pressing it into the edges. Transfer it to the oven and bake at 180C/360F for 15-20 minutes. Remove them from the oven and allow them to cool before cutting into bars. Place the chocolate into a bowl and place it over a saucepan of gently simmering water until it melts. Dip each bar into dark chocolate then transfer them to the fridge. Enjoy.

Fresh Raspberry Protein Bars

MAKES 12-14

Ingredients

125g (4oz) peanut butter

175g (6oz) oats

75g (3oz) raspberries

50g (2oz) linseeds (flaxseeds)

2 teaspoons stevia

Method

Place the oats, peanut butter and stevia, linseeds (flaxseeds) into a food processor and process until smooth. Stir in the raspberries. Spoon the mixture into a small baking tin and smooth it out. Chill in the fridge for 2 hours until the mixture has set. Cut it into bars and eat straight away or store them in the fridge. You could try substituting the raspberries for blueberries or chopped strawberries and unsweetened chocolate chips.

Coconut & Cranberry Flapjacks

MAKES 12

Ingredients

200g (7oz) oats

50g (2oz) desiccated (shredded) coconut

50g (2oz) unsweetened dried cranberries

2 tablespoons almond butter

1 tablespoon coconut oil

2 teaspoons stevia sweetener

1 teaspoon vanilla extract

Method

Place the coconut oil, almond butter, stevia and vanilla extract into a saucepan and warm it gently whilst stirring. In a large bowl, mix together the oats and coconut. Pour the melted ingredients into the oats and combine them together. Add the cranberries and mix well. Grease and line a baking tin with greaseproof paper. Spoon the mixture into the baking tin and smooth it down. Transfer it to the oven and bake at 200C/400F for 12-14 minutes or until slightly golden. Allow it to cool before cutting into slices.

Cookie Dough Bars

Ingredients

100g (3½oz) oats
75g (3oz) almond nut butter
2 teaspoons vanilla extract
1-2 teaspoons stevia (optional)
150mls (5fl oz) almond milk

MAKES 9

Method

Place the oats into a food processor and blitz until they become like flour. Add in the stevia (optional) and mix well. Add the almond butter, vanilla and half of the milk and pulse the mixture in the food processor. Gradually add in the remaining milk until it becomes a dough-like consistency. Grease and line a baking tray. Scoop the mixture into the baking tray and smooth it down. Cover and chill for at least 3 hours. Cut the mixture into bars. Serve and enjoy. For a variation to this recipe you can add some raw cocoa chips or drizzle with melted dark chocolate.

Peanut Butter & Banana Flapjacks

Ingredients

250g (9oz) rolled oats

3 tablespoons 100% cocoa powder

2 ripe bananas, mashed

2 tablespoons crunchy peanut butter

1 teaspoon ground cinnamon

Pinch of sea salt

MAKES 8

Method

Place the oats, cocoa powder, cinnamon and salt into a bowl and mix well. Add in the mashed banana and peanut butter and combine all of the ingredients. Spoon the mixture into a shallow baking tin and press the mixture into the sides, smoothing it down. Cover and transfer it to the fridge to chill for 1 hour. Cut it into slices and serve.

Nutty Protein Balls

Ingredients

250g (9oz) ground almonds (almond flour/almond meal)

75g (3oz) desiccated (shredded) coconut

3 tablespoons chia seeds

4 tablespoons 100% cocoa powder

1 banana, mashed

1 tablespoon coconut oil

½ teaspoon vanilla extract

Pinch of salt

MAKES 12

Method

Place the chia seeds in a large bowl with 2 tablespoons of water and let it sit for around 15 minutes until it thickens. Place the chia mixture into a bowl and add all of the other ingredients and combine them well until the mixture is well blended and thick. Using a teaspoon, scoop out the mixture and roll it in your (clean) hands to shape it into balls. Place the balls on a baking sheet and cook them at 190C/375F for 15 minutes.

Chocolate Coconut & Almond Bars

MAKES 16

Ingredients

200g (7oz) desiccated (shredded) unsweetened coconut

200g (7oz) ground almonds (almond meal/almond flour)

1 large ripe banana

2 tablespoons melted coconut oil

FOR THE TOPPING:

100g (3½ oz) unsweetened chocolate chips or cacao nibs

flesh of 1 large avocado

2-3 teaspoons stevia sweetener

2 teaspoons coconut oil

1 teaspoon vanilla extract

Method

Place the banana, coconut, coconut oil and almonds into a food processor and mix until soft. Grease and line a baking tin with parchment paper. Spoon the mixture into the tin and place it in the fridge to chill. Put the chocolate chips/cacao nibs into a bowl. Place the bowl over a saucepan of hot water and stir until they've melted. Place the avocado flesh, stevia, coconut oil and vanilla in the blender and process until creamy. Pour the chocolate in and combine it with the avocado mixture. Once the base has chilled scoop the filling onto it and smooth it out. Cover and chill until completely set. Cut it into bars and keep it in the fridge until ready to serve.

Chocolate Balls

Ingredients

225g (8oz) chopped walnuts

150g (5oz) dates (pitted)

4 tablespoons 100% cocoa powder

2 tablespoons water

1 teaspoon vanilla extract

Pinch of salt

Extra cocoa powder for coating

MAKES 12

Method

Place all of the ingredients into a food processor and mix until soft and creamy. Scoop out a spoonful of the mixture and using clean hands, shape it into a ball. Repeat for the remaining mixture. Sprinkle some cocoa powder onto a plate and roll the balls in it go give them a nice even chocolate dusting. Chill before serving.

Chocolate Coated Almond Bars

Ingredients

FOR THE BASE:

200g (7oz) almonds
200g (7oz) desiccated (shredded) coconut
2 small ripe bananas
1/2 teaspoon sea salt
2 tablespoon coconut oil, melted

FOR THE CHOCOLATE LAYER:

100g (3½ oz) dark chocolate (min 70% cacao)
1 avocado
1-2 tablespoons stevia sweetener or to taste
1 teaspoon coconut oil
1 teaspoon vanilla extract

MAKES 16

Method

Place the coconut and almonds into a food processor and blitz until they are finely ground. Add the banana, coconut oil and salt and combine until the mixture soft and doughy. Line a baking tin with greaseproof paper and press the mixture into the tin, spreading it into the edges. Transfer it to the fridge to chill. In the meantime, place the chocolate into a bowl and place it over a saucepan of gently simmering water until it melts. Place the avocado, stevia, coconut oil and vanilla in the blend and process until creamy. Pour the chocolate in and combine it with the avocado mixture. Take the chilled base mixture from the fridge and smooth on the chocolate topping. Cover the tin and return it to the fridge until the chocolate has set. Cut it into bars. Enjoy.

Apple Pie Energy Bars

Ingredients

175g (6oz) oats
125g (4oz) almond butter/smooth peanut butter
100g (3½oz) ground almonds (almond flour/almond meal)
3 large apples, peeled, cored and finely chopped
1½ teaspoons ground cinnamon
1 teaspoon ground mixed spice
1 teaspoon ground nutmeg
1-2 teaspoons stevia sweetener
5 tablespoons water

MAKES 12

Method

Place the apples in a saucepan with five tablespoons of water. Gently warm the apples until they soften to a pulp then remove them from the heat and allow to cool. Place the oats, ground almonds (almond meal/almond flour) and spices in a large bowl and mix well. Place the almond butter and stevia together in a bowl and warm them in the microwave until it has melted. Combine the nut butter mixture with the dry ingredients and mix well. Add in the cooked apple and mix thoroughly. Line a baking tin and scoop the mixture into it, pressing it into the sides. Cover and chill for 30 minutes. Cut into slices and serve.

Chickpea & Chocolate Chip Blondies

MAKES 12

Ingredients

400g (14oz) tin of chickpeas (garbanzo beans), drained

75g (3oz) smooth peanut butter or cashew butter

50g (2oz) unsweetened chocolate chips or cacao nibs

1 tablespoons raw honey

1 ripe banana

1 teaspoon vanilla extract

1/2 teaspoon baking soda

100% cocoa powder for sprinkling (optional)

Method

Place all of the ingredients, apart from the cacao nibs/chocolate chips, into a food processor and mix until it becomes a smooth consistency. Stir in the chocolate chips. Grease and line a square baking tin and spoon the mixture into the tin. Transfer it to the oven and bake at 180C/360F for around 20 minutes. Test the mixture with a skewer which should come out clean when cooked. Sprinkle with cocoa powder (optional). Allow it to cool before cutting it into bars.

Snowy Coconut Balls

Ingredients

125g (4oz) almond butter
75g (3oz) macadamia nuts, chopped
75g (3oz) desiccated (shredded) coconut
2 tablespoons tahini paste
1 teaspoon vanilla extract
1 teaspoon stevia sweetener (or more to taste)
Extra coconut for coating

MAKES 24

Method

Place the coconut, tahini, almond butter, vanilla extract and chopped macadamia nuts into a bowl and combine them thoroughly. Stir in a teaspoon of stevia powder then taste to check the sweetness. Add a little more sweetener if you wish. Roll the mixture into balls. Scatter some desiccated (shredded) coconut on a plate and coat the balls in it. Keep them refrigerated until ready to use.

Creamy Avocado Chocolate Bites

Ingredients

- 75g (6oz) dark chocolate, minimum 80% cocoa or cacao nibs
- 3 avocados, flesh removed
- 1 teaspoon vanilla extract
- 1 tablespoon honey (or 1/2-1 teaspoon stevia powder) (optional)
- 100% cocoa powder for rolling
- Pinch of salt

MAKES 14 approx.

Method

Place the chocolate in a large bowl and place it over a saucepan of gently simmering water until the chocolate has melted. Add in the vanilla, salt, honey or stevia (if using) and stir. Mash the avocado until it is smooth and creamy. Pour the melted chocolate into the avocado and mix it thoroughly. Chill in the fridge for 30 minutes until it becomes thicker. Using a teaspoon, scoop out the mixture and roll it into balls. Place the cocoa powder for rolling on a plate and completely coat the chocolate balls in the mixture. Serve and enjoy.

Chilli Chocolate Bites

Ingredients

125g (4oz) finely milled oats

50g (2oz) cacao nibs or unsweetened chocolate chips

3 teaspoons stevia powder (or to taste)

2 tablespoons 100% cocoa powder

1 teaspoon ground cinnamon

3 tablespoons coconut oil, melted

2 tablespoons water

1 teaspoon vanilla extract

1/4 teaspoon cayenne pepper

Pinch of salt

MAKES 16

Method

Place the oats, cayenne pepper, ground cinnamon, stevia, salt and cocoa powder into a bowl and mix well. Stir in the coconut oil, water and vanilla extract and combine all of the ingredients. Stir in the chocolate chips/cacao nibs. Grease and line a baking sheet. Scoop out a spoonful of the mixture, shape it into a ball and flatten it down on the baking sheet. Repeat for the remaining mixture. Place them in the oven and bake at 170C/325F for 12 minutes. Allow them to cool before serving.

Desserts & Puddings

Banana & Blueberry Pudding

Ingredients

150g (5oz) risotto rice
100g (3½oz) fresh blueberries
1 large ripe banana
1 vanilla pod, cut open
1 litre (1¾ pints) almond milk

SERVES 4

Method

Pour the almond milk into saucepan and add the rice, banana and vanilla pod. Bring it to the boil then reduce the heat and simmer for 15 minutes until the rice is cooked through and soft. Remove the vanilla pod and stir in the blueberries. Serve the pudding immediately.

Creamy Rice Pudding

Ingredients

125g (4oz) risotto rice
50g (2oz) hazelnuts, chopped
50g (2oz) almonds, chopped
50g (2oz) butter
2 teaspoons stevia sweetener
1 teaspoon ground cinnamon
600mls (1 pint) warm milk

SERVES 4

Method

Heat a frying pan, add the chopped nuts and toast until golden, then set aside. Heat the butter in a saucepan, stir in the rice and cook for around 1 minute. Slowly add the warm milk to the rice, stirring continuously. Add the stevia and cinnamon and simmer gently for around 20 minutes until the rice is soft. Serve the rice pudding into bowls and sprinkle with the toasted nuts.

Raspberry & Passion Fruit Swirl

Ingredients

400g (14oz) mascarpone cheese
275g (10oz) raspberries
Seeds of 2 passion fruit
A few extra raspberries to garnish

SERVES 4

Method

Place the raspberries in a bowl and mash them to a pulp. In a separate bowl, stir the seeds from the passion fruit into the mascarpone and mix well. Take decorative glasses or dessert bowls and spoon a layer of the mascarpone in then add a spoonful of the raspberry purée and swirl it slightly, repeat with another layer of mascarpone and raspberry until the mixture has been used up. Garnish with a few raspberries and chill before serving.

Apple & Walnut Creams

Ingredients

100g (3½oz) cream cheese
50g (2oz) walnuts, roughly chopped
4 apples
½ teaspoon ground cinnamon
3 tablespoons lemon juice

**SERVES
4**

Method

Peel and core the apples then slice them evenly width ways to create a circular shape. Lightly coat the apple slices in lemon juice and place them on a serving plate. Mix together the cream cheese, cinnamon and walnuts then spoon a little of the mixture onto each apple ring. Eat immediately.

Ricotta Stuffed Peaches

Ingredients

100g (3½oz) ricotta
4 large ripe peaches, halved and stone removed
2 tablespoons oat bran
Zest and juice of 1 orange

SERVES
4

Method

Place the peaches in an oven-proof dish with the flat side facing up. Place the orange zest a
juice, oat bran and ricotta cheese into a bowl and combine the ingredients. Spoon the crea
mixture into the centre of the peaches. Bake them in the oven at 180C/360F for 15 minute
Serve them on their own or with a little crème fraîche or plain yogurt.

Strawberry Fool

Ingredients

350g (12oz) strawberries
175mls (6fl oz) plain unflavoured yogurt
175mls (6fl oz) whipping cream (heavy cream)
or crème fraîche
1 teaspoon stevia (optional)
A few extra strawberries to garnish

SERVES 4

Method

Place the strawberries into a blender and puree them. If you require extra sweetness mix in the stevia powder. Push the strawberry purée through a sieve to remove all of the seeds. Whip the cream until thick then combine it with the yogurt. Mix the strawberry purée with the cream and yogurt. Spoon the dessert into decorative glasses and top with a few strawberries. Chill before serving.

Rhubarb & Ginger Fool

Ingredients

450g (1lb) rhubarb, thickly chopped
150g (5oz) Greek yoghurt
3 teaspoons stevia sweetener
1 teaspoon ground cinnamon
1 teaspoon ground ginger
50mls (2fl oz) freshly squeezed orange juice

SERVES 6

Method

Place the orange juice, rhubarb, cinnamon, ginger and stevia into a saucepan and cook for 10-15 minutes until the rhubarb has softened. Remove from the heat and allow it to cool. Swirl the yogurt into the rhubarb mixture. Spoon it into dessert bowls or glasses and chill before serving.

Strawberry & Coconut Flan

Ingredients

FOR THE BASE:

100g (3½oz) hazelnuts

100g (3½oz) cashew nuts

3 teaspoons stevia sweetener

2 teaspoons water

1 teaspoon vanilla extract

FOR THE TOPPING:

175g (6oz) ripe strawberries

100g cashew nuts

50g (2oz) desiccated coconut

4 teaspoons stevia sweetener

75g (3oz) coconut oil, melted

1 teaspoon vanilla extract

A few strawberries to garnish

SERVES 10

Method

Place the nuts and stevia into a blender and process until soft and smooth. Add in the vanilla extract and water and mix until it begins to stick together. Transfer the mixture to a flan tin and place it in the fridge for 45 minutes to allow it to firm up. Place the cashew nuts, strawberries, desiccated coconut, coconut oil, stevia and vanilla extract into a food processor and mix until smooth. Spoon the strawberry mixture onto the flan base. Chill in the fridge for at least an hour and serve with a few strawberries scattered on top.

Pecan & Apple Pie

Ingredients

250g (9oz) pecan nuts

8 apples, peeled, cored and finely sliced

1½ teaspoons ground cinnamon

1 tablespoon butter

1 teaspoon vanilla extract

2 tablespoons water

Pinch of salt

SERVES 6

Method

Place the nuts, cinnamon, butter, vanilla, salt and water into a food processor and blitz until smooth. Spoon the mixture into a pie dish and smooth it down. Transfer it to the oven and bake at 190C/375F for around 10 minutes. Remove it from the oven. Cover the base with the apple slices and a sprinkling of cinnamon (optional). Reduce the oven temperature to 180C/360F. Cover the pie with foil, place it in the oven and cook for around 45 minutes. Serve with a dollop of whipped cream or crème fraîche. Enjoy.

Spiced Poached Peaches

Ingredients

4 star anise
4 large peaches
2 cinnamon sticks
300mls (½ pint) water
2 teaspoons stevia sweetener

SERVES 4

Method

Place the stevia and water in a saucepan and bring to the boil. Add the peaches, star anise and cinnamon sticks. Reduce the heat and simmer gently for 10 minutes. Remove the peaches, cover to keep them warm and set aside. Continue cooking the liquid for another 5 minutes. Serve the peaches with the liquid drizzled over the top.

Chocolate Mousse

Ingredients

150mls (6fl oz) double cream (heavy cream)
100g (3½oz) cream cheese such as mascarpone or ricotta
2 tablespoons butter
2 tablespoons 100% cocoa powder
2 teaspoon stevia (or to taste)

SERVES 4

Method

Place the butter and stevia into a bowl and mix well. Stir in the cream cheese and cocoa powder and mix thoroughly. Whip the cream until thick and fold it into the mixture. Spoon the mousse into dessert bowls and chill before serving.

Summer Pudding

Ingredients

450g (1lb) strawberries, stalks removed
450g (1lb) raspberries
2 teaspoons stevia sweetener (optional)
6 slices of thick bread

SERVES 6-8

Method

Place the strawberries and raspberries into a saucepan, together with the stevia (if using) and heat gently until the fruit has softened. Remove and set aside. Using a large bowl, place the bread slices around the bowl, completely lining it so that there are no gaps. You may need to slice the bread into smaller pieces to make it fit. Spoon the fruit into the bowl. Place a plate that fits just inside the bowl and press it down. Place it in the fridge for around 1 hour making sure it is completely chilled before turning out and serving. Serve with a dollop of cream.

Mango Ice Cream

Ingredients

3 ripe mangoes, de-stoned and peeled
600mls (1 pint) double cream (heavy cream)
Juice of 1 lime

**SERVES
6**

Method

Place the mango into a food processor and blitz until smooth. Add in the cream and lime juice and process until smooth and creamy. Transfer the mixture to an airtight container and place it in the freezer. Whisk with a fork after 1-2 hours and continue to freeze. Alternatively pour the mixture into an ice cream maker and follow the manufacturer's instructions.

'Real' Custard

Ingredients

4 egg yolks
1 egg
1 tablespoon stevia sweetener
1 teaspoon vanilla extract
1 teaspoon cornflour
600mls (1 pint) full fat milk
100mls (3½ fl oz) double cream (heavy cream)

SERVES 4

Method

Take a large bowl and beat your egg yolks and egg. Add your stevia sweetener and cornflour and mix well. Pour the milk into a saucepan along with the vanilla extract. Bring it to the boil. Slowly add the hot milk to the egg mixture and stir well. Pour back into a large pan with your cream and stir until thickened. Enjoy with a hot or cold dessert.

Chocolate Lava Pots

SERVES 2

Ingredients

100g (3½ oz) cacao nibs or
85% cocoa chocolate
50g (2oz) butter
25g (1oz) coconut flour
2 large eggs (beaten)
2 teaspoons stevia
25mls (1floz) milk

Method

Grease 2 ramekin dishes with a little butter. Place the chocolate, stevia and butter in a bowl and place it over a saucepan of gently simmering water. Place the coconut flour in a bowl and stir in the beaten eggs. Warm the milk to just before it starts to simmer. Slowly pour the milk into the egg mixture and whisk continuously. Stir the chocolate mixture into the flour mixture. Spoon the mixture into the ramekin dishes. Transfer them to the oven and cook at 200C/400F for 12-14 minutes. Serve and eat straight away. The centre should be liquid chocolate. Enjoy.

Profiteroles

Ingredients

FOR THE PROFITEROLE:

75g (3oz) plain flour (all-purpose flour), sieved

50g (2oz) butter (unsalted)

2 teaspoons stevia sweetener

2 eggs, beaten

60mls (2fl oz) cold water

FOR THE FILLING:

250mls (8fl oz) whipping cream

1 teaspoon vanilla extract

1 teaspoon stevia sweetener (optional)

FOR THE CHOCOLATE TOPPING:

2 tablespoons 100% cocoa powder

2 teaspoons stevia sweetener (or to taste)

60mls (2fl oz) double cream (heavy cream)

1 teaspoon vanilla extract

**MAKES
20 approx.**

Method

Place the flour in a bowl with the stevia sweetener, mix and set aside. Place the water and butter in a saucepan, bring it to the boil and remove from the heat. Whisk in the flour, until it forms a thick paste. Add the egg, stirring constantly until smooth. Scoop out the mixture using a teaspoon and place them onto a baking tray lined with parchment paper until you've used up all of the mixture. Transfer to the oven and bake at 200C/400F and cook for 10 minutes, then increase the temperature to 220C/440F and cook for another 5 minutes. Prick each profiterole with a thin skewer to let the moisture out and allow them to cool completely. Whisk up the cream, vanilla extract and stevia (if using) and set aside. Place the cream, cocoa powder, stevia and vanilla extract into a saucepan and warm it gently, stirring constantly. Set aside for it to cool down. Cut each profiterole almost in half, place a teaspoon of cream into it and replace the lid. Coat each profiterole in some of the sauce. Serve and eat immediately.

Chocolate Orange Ice Cream

Ingredients

200g (8oz) 100% cocoa powder
3 teaspoons stevia powder
Zest and juice of 2 oranges
600mls (1 pint) double cream (heavy cream)

SERVES
6

Method

Place the cocoa powder and stevia in a bowl and stir in the cream. Add in the orange zest and juice and mix thoroughly. Transfer the mixture to an ice-cream maker and follow the manufacturer's instructions. Alternatively, pour the mixture into an airtight container and place it in the freezer. Whisk it with a fork after freezing for around an hour then return it to the freezer once more.

Apple & Blackberry Pie

Ingredients

FOR THE PIE CRUST:
400g (14oz) plain flour (all-purpose flour)
200g (7oz) butter or margarine
1 tablespoon water

FOR THE FILLING:
250g (9oz) blackberries
250g (9oz) sweet apples
2-3 teaspoons stevia sweetener (optional if
the fruit is very sweet)
1 teaspoon ground cinnamon
1/2 teaspoon ground nutmeg
125mls (4fl oz) warm water

SERVES 8

Method

Place the flour into a bowl, add the butter and using clean fingers, rub the flour into the butter until it is partially bound together. Stir in the water to bind the pastry together. Roll out half of the pastry onto a floured surface. Grease a pie dish and place the pastry over the dish, trimming any excess from around the dish. Bake the pastry blind in an oven preheated to 200C/400F for 5 minutes. In the meantime, place the blackberries, apples, cinnamon, nutmeg and stevia (if using) into a saucepan and pour in the water. Cook for around 5 minutes, stirring occasionally. Scoop the filling into the prepared pie crust. Roll out the rest of the pastry, cover the filling and trim off any excess. Place the pie in the oven and cook for around 20 minutes or until slightly golden. Serve with sugar-free 'real' custard or cream.

Rhubarb Crumble

Ingredients

FOR THE FILLING
675g (1½lb) fresh rhubarb, leaves removed and chopped

3 teaspoons stevia sweetener (or to taste)

FOR THE CRUMBLE:
100g (3½oz) plain flour (all-purpose flour)

100g (3½oz) butter

2 teaspoons stevia sweetener

SERVES 6

Method

Place the rhubarb into a saucepan and pour in just enough water to cover it. Bring it to the boil, reduce the heat and simmer for 5 minutes until it begins to soften. Stir in 3 teaspoons of stevia and set aside. Place the flour in a bowl and stevia into a bowl and stir. Rub in the butter until it becomes crumbly. Spoon the rhubarb into a large ovenproof dish and scatter the crumble over the top. Transfer it to the oven, preheated to 200C/400F and cook for around 15 minutes or until golden. Remove it from the oven and serve it with a swirl of cream. Delicious!

Avocado & Melon Salad

Ingredients

2 large ripe avocados, sliced
1 cantaloupe melon, cubed
½ teaspoon ground ginger
Juice of 1 lemon

SERVES 4

Method

Mix the lemon juice and ginger together in a bowl. Add the avocados and melon and toss gently. Chill before serving.

Sweet
Treats

Toasted Brazil Nut Truffles

Ingredients

200g (7oz) toasted coconut flakes
100g (3½oz) Brazil nuts, chopped
2 teaspoons vanilla extract
2 tablespoons coconut oil

SERVES 4

Method

Place all of the ingredients into a blender and process until smooth and creamy. Add a little extra coconut oil if required. Divide the mixture into bite-size pieces and roll it into balls. Place the balls into small paper cake cases. Chill before serving.

Chocolate & Bean Fudge

Ingredients

MAKES
20 approx.

- 400g (14oz) tin of black beans, rinsed and drained
- 75g (3oz) 100% cocoa powder
- 50g (2oz) cacao nibs or unsweetened chocolate chips
- 2 egg whites
- Flesh of 1 ripe avocado
- 1 large egg
- 1/2 teaspoon bicarbonate of soda
- 2 teaspoons vanilla extract
- 3 teaspoons stevia sweetener
- 1 teaspoon coconut oil

Method

Place all of the ingredients, except the cacao nibs/chocolate chips, into a blender and process until soft and smooth. Stir in the cacao nibs/chocolate chips. Grease and line a baking tin with parchment paper. Spoon the mixture into the tin. Transfer it to the oven and bake at 180C/360F for around 25 minutes. Allow the fudge to cool. Cut it into squares. Store in an airtight container until ready to use.

Cinnamon Truffles

Ingredients

150g (6oz) hazelnuts
100g (3½oz) pitted dates
25g (1oz) desiccated (shredded) unsweetened coconut
3 tablespoons 100% cocoa powder
1 teaspoon ground cinnamon
½ teaspoon ground ginger
1 tablespoon coconut oil
1-2 tablespoons water (optional)

MAKES
14

Method

Place the nuts into a food processor and blend until they become fine. Add in the remaining ingredients and blitz them until soft and sticky. Try adding a spoonful or two of water if the mixture seems too thick. Using clean hands, shape the mixture into balls. Chill before serving.

Peach & Raspberry Ice Lollies

SERVES 6

Ingredients

- 4 ripe peaches, de-stoned
- 8 raspberries, halved
- 1 banana, peeled
- 1 teaspoon lemon juice

Method

Gently drop the peaches in a saucepan of hot water and remove after around 20 seconds and place them into a bowl of cold water. Remove the skin from the peaches which will have now loosened. Place the peaches, banana and lemon juice in a blender and blitz until smooth. Stir in the raspberries pieces. Pour the mixture into ice lolly moulds and insert the sticks. Transfer to the freezer until set.

Chocolate Crispie Cakes

Ingredients

150g (5oz) rice puffs (sugar-free)
100g (3½ oz) 100% cocoa powder
3 tablespoons butter
3 teaspoons stevia powder (or to taste)

SERVES 4

Method

Place the butter and stevia into a saucepan and warm it until it melts. Stir in the cocoa powder and mix thoroughly. Add the rice puffs to the chocolate and coat them completely. Spoon the mixture into individual cupcake papers. Allow to cool before serving.

Nut Brittle

Ingredients

175g (6oz) 100% cocoa powder

25g (1oz) butter

25g (1oz) whole hazelnuts

25g (1oz) Brazil nuts

3 teaspoons stevia powder (or to taste)

SERVES 4

Method

Place the butter in a saucepan along with the stevia and stir until melted. Stir in the cocoa powder and mix well. Stir in the nuts and mix well to coat them completely. Spread the nuts on a greased baking sheet. Transfer it to the fridge and chill for around 1 hour or until set. Chop it into rough chunks. Enjoy.

Banana & Choc Chip Frozen Yogurt

SERVES
6-8

Ingredients

900g (2lb) plain Greek yogurt
50g (2oz) cacao nibs or unsweetened
chocolate chips
4 large ripe bananas
4 teaspoons stevia powder
1 teaspoon vanilla extract

Method

Place the bananas, yogurt, stevia and vanilla extract into a food processor and mix until smooth and creamy. Stir in the cacao nibs/unsweetened chocolate chips. Transfer the mixture to an ice cream maker and freeze the yogurt according to the manufacturer's instructions. Alternatively, pour the yogurt into a container and freeze it for one hour. Remove it and whisk with a fork. Return it to the freezer and whisk again after another hour and continue until completely set. Serve and enjoy.

Cherry Chocolate Milkshake

Ingredients

Flesh of ½ avocado
75g (3oz) frozen cherries
1 tablespoon 100% cocoa powder
100mls (3½ fl oz) milk or almond milk

SERVES 1

Method

Place all of the ingredients into a food processor and blitz until smooth and creamy. Pour it into a tall glass and serve.

Tropical Ice Cream Lollies

Ingredients

1 pineapple, peeled and chopped
200mls (7fl oz) coconut milk

MAKES
12 approx.

Method

Place the pineapple and coconut into a food processor and process until it's really smooth and creamy. Pour the mixture into ice lolly moulds. Place them in the freezer until completely set. Keep in the freezer until ready to use.

Strawberry Jam

Ingredients

375g (13oz) strawberries, stalk removed
25g (1oz) chia seeds
4 teaspoons stevia sweetener

Method

Place the strawberries into a food processor and blitz until smooth. Place the strawberries to a bowl and stir in the stevia and chia seeds and mix well. Cover the bowl and place it in the fridge for 2 ½ hours. Spoon the strawberry mixture into a food processor and mix until jam-like. Transfer the mixture to a clean jam-jar and cover it. Store the jam in the fridge.

Sweet Sugar-Free Popcorn

Ingredients

- 100g (3½ oz) unpopped popcorn
- 2 teaspoons butter or coconut oil
- 1 teaspoon stevia sweetener

Method

Place the butter/oil and stevia into a large saucepan and gently warm it while stirring. Turn the heat up high. Add the uncooked popcorn and place a lid on the saucepan. Cook for around 2-3 minutes or until all the corn has popped. Allow it to cool before serving.

Cinnamon Coconut Chips

Ingredients

175g (6oz) unsweetened coconut flakes
1 teaspoon cinnamon
1/2 teaspoon stevia sweetener (optional)

SERVES 4

Method

Scatter the coconut flakes onto a baking sheet. Sprinkle the cinnamon and stevia (if using) over the coconut. Transfer them to the oven and cook at 170C/325F for around 5 minutes until the coconut is slightly golden. Allow them to cool. Serve and enjoy.

Sweet Chilli Peanuts

SERVES 4-6

Ingredients

275g (10oz) unsalted peanuts
25g (1oz) butter
2 teaspoons stevia sweetener
½ teaspoon cayenne pepper
Pinch of salt

Method

Place the butter in a bowl and beat in the stevia, cayenne pepper and salt. Line a baking sheet with greaseproof paper. Stir the peanuts into the butter mixture and coat them well. Spread them onto the baking sheet. Transfer them to the oven and cook at 180C/360F and roast them for 10 minutes, giving them a stir half-way through. Allow them to cool before serving.

You may also be interested in other titles by
Erin Rose Publishing
which are available in both paperback and ebook.

 Quick Start Guides

GAR FREE DIET — SUGAR FREE DIET COOKBOOK — SUGAR FREE FAMILY COOKBOOK — DAIRY FREE DIET — DIABETES DIET COOKBOOK — ALKALINE DIET SOLUTION

          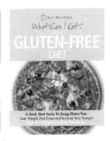

LOOD SUGAR DIET RECIPE BOOK — BLOOD SUGAR DIET Recipes For Life — BLOOD SUGAR DIET Family Favourites — BLOOD SUGAR DIET COOKBOOK — SIRT FOOD DIET RECIPE BOOK — GLUTEN-FREE DIET

LOWER CHOLESTEROL DIET — LOW CARB HIGH FAT DIET — LOW CARB HIGH FAT DIET COOKBOOK — Low FODMAP Diet COOKBOOK

Books by Sophie Ryan
Erin Rose Publishing

30 Simple And Delicious Superfood Energy Balls And Bites
Recipes For Great Health and Wellbeing

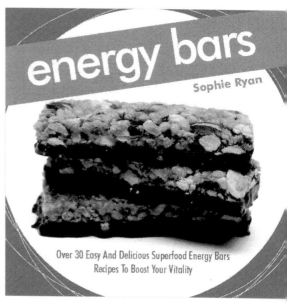

Over 30 Easy And Delicious Superfood Energy Bars
Recipes To Boost Your Vitality

30 Simple And Tasty Energy Shots And Smoothies
To Power Up Your Health And Well-Being